THE NATURE KIDS GUIDE TO
BOBCATS

DAVID ANDERSON

LP Media Inc. Publishing
Text copyright © 2026 by LP Media Inc.

For information address LP Media Inc. Publishing,
30012 Variolite St NW, Princeton MN 55371
www.lpmedia.org

Publication Data

Bobcats
The Nature Kid's Guide to Bobcats — First edition.

Summary: "Learn all about Bobcats, the Nature Kid Way"
— Provided by publisher.

ISBN: 979-8-89818-121-5

[1. Bobcats - Non-Fiction] I. Title.

Title: The Nature Kid's Guide to Bobcats

CONTENTS

WILD WOODS
DID YOU KNOW?
Bobcats are named for their short, bobbed tails. A shorter tail helps them sneak through thick bushes without getting stuck.

4

Growl! A bobcat crouches in the bushes. Its spotted fur blends in perfectly.

Bobcats live in many kinds of places. They make their homes in forests, swamps, deserts, and near mountains.

These wild cats need places to hide. They rest in hollow logs and rocky dens. Thick brush gives them cover too.

Bobcats like areas with lots of trees and bushes. The plants help them stay out of sight. This makes hunting easier.

Bobcats often live close to people. Some make dens near farms and towns. They come out at night when it is quiet and dark.

BACKYARD BOBCATS

Rustle! A bobcat walks through tall grass near a house.

Bobcats live in North America. They roam from Canada to Mexico.

These cats can look different from place to place. Some have darker fur. Others have lighter coats.

These cats live across the United States. They live in almost every state. Only Alaska, Delaware, and Hawaii have no bobcats. This makes the bobcat the most common wild cat in the country.

Texas has more bobcats than any other state. Over 200,000 of them live there!

SMALL BUT
STRONG

Thump! A bobcat lands on a log. It looks around slowly.

Bobcats are medium-sized wild cats. They weigh between 15 and 35 pounds, with males usually bigger than females.

These cats stand about 20 inches tall at the shoulder. That makes them roughly twice the size of a house cat.

Bobcats are very strong for their size. Their strong muscles help them catch **prey** bigger than themselves.

Bobcats have even been known to hunt and take down small deer!

BUILT TOUGH

DID YOU KNOW?
Bobcats can rotate each ear separately to hear sounds from different directions.

Snap! A bobcat stretches its back legs on a branch.

Bobcats have bodies built for hunting. Their back legs are longer than their front legs. This helps them jump and run fast.

Thick fur covers their whole body. It keeps them warm in cold weather. Their thick fur also protects them from rain and dirt.

Bobcats have strong jaws and sharp teeth. Their teeth can bite through tough meat and bone. Curved claws help them grip prey tightly.

Padded paws let bobcats walk quietly. They can sneak up on animals without making a sound.

SUPER SENSES

Screech! A bobcat turns its ears toward a sound. What did it hear?

Bobcats have amazing senses. Their large eyes see well in dim light. This helps them hunt at dawn and dusk.

Their ears twist in different directions. Each ear moves on its own. This helps bobcats find sounds all around them.

Bobcats also have a strong sense of smell. They can follow the trail of an animal that passed by hours before.

All these senses make bobcats great hunters.

Bobcats can see six times better than humans in the dark.

HIDDEN
HUNTER

Snarl! A bobcat hides behind a rock. Its eyes watch closely.

Bobcats are great at hiding. Their spotted coats help them blend in. They can hide well in forests, deserts, and rocky areas.

These cats stay very still. They do this when danger is near. They crouch low to the ground. Their fur pattern breaks up their shape.

Bobcats also use shadows. They rest in thick brush. They rest under fallen trees. This keeps them safe from enemies.

Bobcats can swim well and catch fish, but they usually prefer to stay dry.

MEATY
MENU

Purrr. A bobcat rests under a shady tree after a large meal. It looks happy.

Bobcats are **carnivores**. This means they only eat meat. They hunt many types of animals.

Rabbits and hares are their favorite meals. Bobcats also catch squirrels, mice, and birds. Sometimes they eat snakes and lizards too.

A hungry bobcat can eat a whole rabbit at once. They hide extra food under leaves. They come back later to eat it.

Bobcats have rough tongues that grab meat and pull it off bones.

POUNCE POWER

Bobcats can wait without moving for over an hour before they pounce on prey.

18

Pounce! A bobcat leaps from behind a bush and lands on its prey in a flash.

Bobcats are sneaky hunters. They do not chase prey for long distances. Instead, they wait and watch quietly.

A bobcat creeps close to its target. It moves slowly and stays low. When the moment is right, it pounces. Their strong back legs help them jump up to ten feet in one leap.

These cats use their sharp claws to grab prey. Most hunts happen in just a few seconds. Their prey often never sees them until it is to late.

WATCH OUT

Hiss! A bobcat spots a coyote. It arches its back to look bigger.

Bobcats are small compared to many other predators. Coyotes, mountain lions, and wolves are bigger than bobcats. These animals can be dangerous.

Mountain lions are a big threat. They weigh up to five times more than a bobcat. Wolves hunt in packs, which makes them strong.

Bobcats climb trees or hide in rocky dens to stay safe. Being small helps them fit into tight spaces.

Great horned owls sometimes swoop down and attack young bobcats from the sky.

QUICK
ESCAPE

Whoosh! A bobcat darts into thick brush. It vanishes fast.

Bobcats know how to escape danger. They run fast when they need to. A scared bobcat can sprint up to thirty miles per hour.

These cats are good at finding hiding spots. They squeeze into hollow logs or rocky cracks. Dense bushes give them cover too.

Bobcats use their sharp senses to detect threats early. They run away before predators get too close.

Bobcats can change direction quickly while running. This helps them dodge larger animals.

LEAP AND CLIMB

Swoosh! A bobcat jumps onto a tree branch and lands softly.

Bobcats are great climbers. Their sharp claws grip bark well. They climb trees to rest or watch for food.

These cats can also leap far. Strong muscles help them spring forward. They jump across streams and over logs.

Bobcats move through rocky areas with ease. They can balance on even narrow ledges.

Bobcats must climb down trees backward. This is because their ankles cannot turn around.

NIGHT PROWLER

Crack! A twig breaks under soft paws. A bobcat is on the hunt at dusk.

Bobcats are most active at dawn and dusk. They have special eyes that see well in low light. This helps them hunt when it is dark.

Scientists call these busy times crepuscular hours. Many prey animals are also active then, which makes hunting easier.

During the day, bobcats often rest. They sleep in dens or shady spots. Hot summer days keep them hidden until evening.

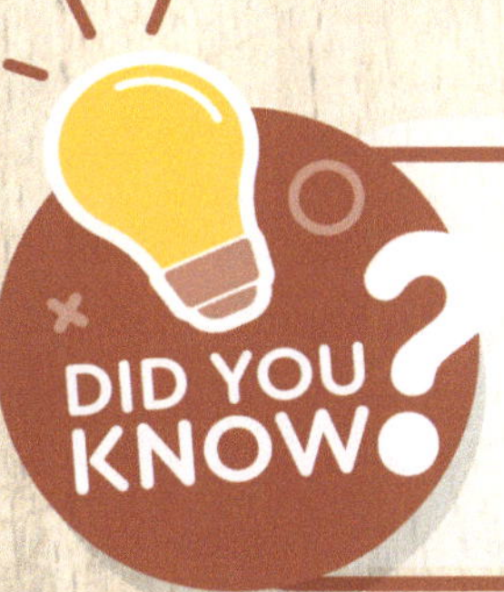

Bobcats are most active in the two hours right after sunset. This is their peak hunting time.

LONE RANGER

Hush! A bobcat walks alone through the quiet forest.

Bobcats live alone most of the time. They do not travel in groups like wolves do.

Each bobcat has its own area called a **home range**. Male bobcats have larger home ranges than females. A male's range may overlap with several females.

Bobcats mark their **territory** with scent. This smell tells other bobcats to stay away.

A male bobcat's range can be 60 square miles. Females have ranges of about 6 miles.

CALLING CATS

Howl! A bobcat calls out in the night. It is mating season.

Bobcats make loud sounds when they want to mate. Males yowl to find females. They also hiss and scream. You can hear these calls from far away.

Mating time is in late winter. Bobcats move around more then. They look for mates.

After mating, the male leaves. The female raises the kittens alone. She finds a safe den in a cave or hollow log. The babies are born there.

Bobcat mating calls can sound like screaming. People often mistake them for a human in distress!

CUTE KITTENS
DID YOU KNOW?
Newborn bobcat kittens weigh between eight and twelve ounces.

Squeak! Tiny bobcat kittens snuggle together in their cozy den.

Bobcat kittens are born with their eyes closed. They cannot see for about ten days. But their fur has spots from the start.

A mother bobcat has one to six kittens at a time. Most litters have two or three kittens. They are born in spring.

Kittens stay in the den for weeks. At first, they drink milk from their mother. Later, she brings them meat to eat.

Young bobcats leave their mother after about one year.

GOOD MOTHERS

34

Grunt! A mother bobcat carries food to her den. Her kittens wait inside.

Mother bobcats work hard to keep kittens safe. They choose hidden dens in rocks or hollow logs. These spots protect babies from weather and danger.

Mothers teach kittens how to hunt. They bring live prey for practice. Kittens learn to stalk and pounce.

As kittens grow, mothers take them on short trips. Young bobcats watch their mother hunt. They copy what she does.

By fall, kittens can catch small animals on their own.

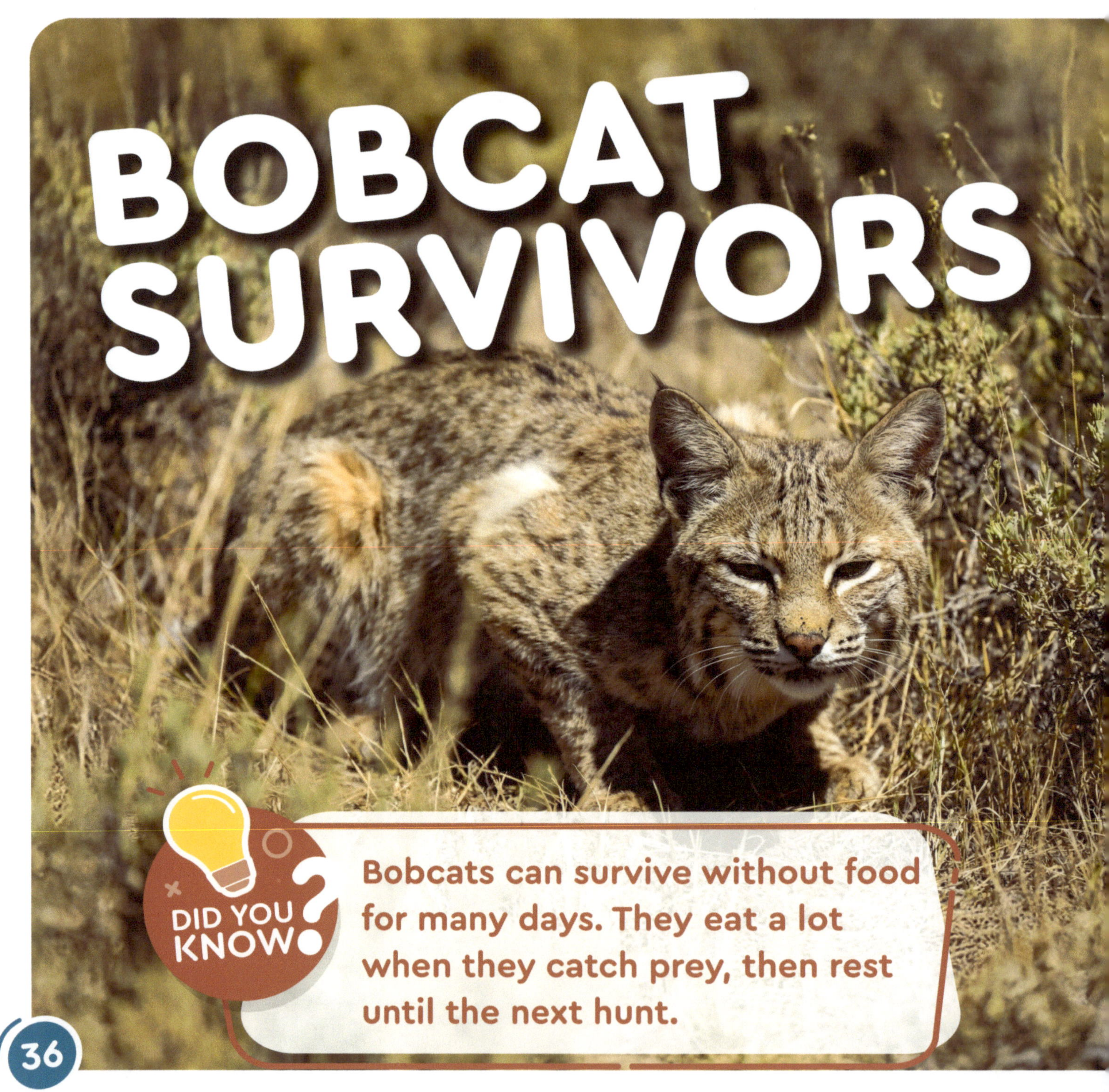

BOBCAT SURVIVORS
DID YOU KNOW?
Bobcats can survive without food for many days. They eat a lot when they catch prey, then rest until the next hunt.

Rustle! A bobcat hides in tall grass. It watches and waits.

Bobcats almost went **extinct** long ago. People hunted them for their fur. Farms and towns took over their land.

But bobcats came back! When forests were cut down, they found new homes. When people moved in, they stayed out of sight

Today, bobcats live closer to people than ever. They hunt in parks and fields near towns. Most people never see them.

More and more bobcats are born each year. They are now the most common wild cat in North America.

BOBCAT SPOTTING

Parks and trails at the edge of town are great spots to look for bobcat tracks.

Rustle! A bobcat walks through a backyard at dusk.

You can be a bobcat spotter! These cats are hard to see. But if you know where to look, you might get lucky and see one.

Go outside at dawn or dusk. Stay very quiet. Look near bushes, logs, and rocky areas. Bobcats like to hide in these spots.

You can also look for clues. Bobcat tracks have four toes and no claw marks. Scratch marks on trees are another sign.

Check near parks, trails, and woods. Bobcats even live near some towns. One might be closer than you think!

GLOSSARY

carnivores
Animals that only eat meat.

extinct
When a type of animal is gone forever. No more of them are alive.

home range
The area where an animal lives and finds its food.

territory
A space that an animal claims as its own.

prey
An animal that is hunted and eaten by another animal.

www.ingramcontent.com/pod-product-compliance
Lightning Source LLC
Chambersburg PA
CBHW041610110726